GEN X

OVERCOMING FEAR & ANXIETY

FINDING YOUR WAY TO HAPPINESS

FLOYD J. SANDERS

TABLE OF CONTENTS

INTRODUCTION

As a member of Generation X, I came of age during a time when our parents, the Baby Boomers, were at the height of their strength and power. We were largely left to be reared by television and music. Our generation was exposed to movies that were violent, news reports of possible war with Russia, and threats of nuclear war at any possible moment. Our future looked bleak, so we came into adulthood, not really believing we would make it to adulthood. Our parents, often absent, either never married, were parenting out of wedlock or were teen parents. We were not parented, provided discipline, or given proper instruction and correction. We raised ourselves!

The prison systems swell with our generation. Our generation populates graveyards. Ours is the generation that makes up most of the homeless population. Drug addiction runs rampant in our generation. Our generation is not called the forgotten generation for nothing. I write this book because, for many years, I have felt that there was something about our generation that sets us apart from those who came before and those who follow. I feel and believe that my generation has a hidden and unrealized potential that, if awakened to and realized, we can transform this world for the better.

Ours is the only generation that remembers the grandparents from the silent generation, one foot in the past, and we have seen the emergence of the internet and all the technologies that followed. Additionally, I feel deeply that there is something hidden in our makeup that, if tapped, will allow us to experience a kind of transformation in consciousness that will change life as we know it for the better.

I write this book to help my generation realize that what has crippled us, preventing us from maximizing our potential, are worry and anxiety. We were saturated with television and other media during our childhood, which caused us to feel and identify with anxiety. We were literally programmed to believe we had no future, and we identified with this by living cautiously, fearfully, and not boldly nor audaciously.

While our Baby Boomer parents maintained control, power, and dominance in government, the market, media, and culture, they literally abandoned us, traumatized us, and belittled us into low self-esteem, drug addiction, and insecurity. It is time for us to awaken, break free of fear, worry, and anxiety, harness our potential, and retire our Baby Boomer parents.

CHAPTER 1: UNDERSTANDING FEAR AND WORRY

The Impact of Fear and Worry on Generation X

Fear and worry have had a profound impact on my generation, often hindering our ability to thrive and reach our full potential. This subchapter delves into the various ways fear and worry manifest in our lives and provides strategies to overcome these obstacles.

One area where fear and worry commonly affect us is in our pursuit of personal goals. Many of us have ambitious aspirations, whether it be excelling in our careers, starting our own businesses, or achieving financial stability. However, fear often holds us back from taking the necessary risks and steps to reach these goals. The fear of failure or the unknown can paralyze our progress, leading to missed opportunities and unfulfilled dreams. Some practical techniques to overcome these fears include reframing failure as a learning experience and setting realistic goals.

Personal finance is another area where fear and worry can wreak havoc on us. Many individuals in our generation have concerns about financial stability, retirement planning, and debt management. These worries can lead to stress, anxiety, and even poor financial decision-making. Some practical strategies to alleviate these worries include creating a budget, seeking professional financial advice, and adopting a mindset of abundance rather than scarcity.

Relationships, both romantic and platonic, can also be significantly impacted by fear and worry for us. Concerns about rejection, abandonment, or the fear of intimacy can prevent us from forming deep and meaningful connections. Some practical ways to overcome these fears include practicing vulnerability, improving communication skills, and seeking therapy or support groups if needed.

For those pursuing entrepreneurial goals, fear and worry can be particularly detrimental. The fear of failure, financial insecurity, or not being taken seriously can deter us from taking the leap into entrepreneurship. Some practical advice to overcome these fears includes building a strong support network, conducting thorough market research, and embracing a growth mindset.

Lastly, fear and worry can also impede our spiritual or personal growth goals. Uncertainty about one's purpose, fear of judgment, or a lack of self-belief can prevent us from embracing our spiritual journey or pursuing personal growth opportunities. Some practical techniques to overcome these fears include meditation, mindfulness practices, seeking spiritual guidance, and connecting with like-minded communities.

In conclusion, fear and worry have had a significant impact on our ability to thrive and reach our goals. However, by recognizing and addressing these fears head-on, we can overcome these obstacles and embrace a life of fulfillment, success, and spiritual transformation.

The Role of Fear and Worry in Hindering Personal Growth

In our journey toward personal growth, fear and worry often act as significant roadblocks. As members of Generation X, we are no strangers to the power these emotions can hold over our lives. In this subchapter, we will explore how fear and worry hinder our progress and discover strategies to overcome them in order to thrive beyond our fears.

Fear and worry have a profound impact on our ability to reach our goals, whether they are related to personal finance, relationships, entrepreneurship, or spiritual and personal growth. These emotions create a sense of uncertainty and doubt, leading us to question our capabilities and hold back from taking the necessary steps toward our aspirations.

When it comes to personal finance goals, fear and worry can paralyze us from making sound financial decisions. We may worry about money, job security, or the fear of failure, preventing us from taking calculated risks or investing in opportunities that could lead to financial growth. By acknowledging and addressing these fears, we can develop a mindset that allows us to make informed decisions, take calculated risks, and ultimately achieve financial success.

Entrepreneurial goals also often suffer due to fear and worry. The fear of failure and the uncertainty of starting a new venture can hold us back from pursuing our entrepreneurial dreams. By embracing a growth mindset, seeking mentorship, and building a support network, we can overcome our fears and take confident steps toward entrepreneurial success.

Finally, fear and worry can hinder our spiritual and personal growth goals. The fear of the unknown or the fear of challenging our existing beliefs may prevent us from exploring our spiritual journey or pursuing personal growth. By acknowledging and embracing these fears, we can open ourselves up to new experiences, beliefs, and transformative growth.

In conclusion, fear and worry play a significant role in hindering personal growth across various aspects of our lives. By understanding the impact these emotions have on our goals, we can develop strategies to overcome them.

Recognizing the Signs and Symptoms of Fear and Worry

In our fast-paced and uncertain world, it is not uncommon for us to experience fear and worry. These emotions can be overwhelming and can hinder our ability to thrive and achieve our goals. However, by recognizing the signs and symptoms of fear and worry, we can take the necessary steps to overcome them and embrace spiritual transformation.

One of the first signs of fear and worry is a constant feeling of unease or anxiety. This may manifest as a racing heart, difficulty sleeping, or a sense of impending doom. Pay attention to these physical symptoms, as they can be indicators of deeper emotional struggles.

Another sign to watch out for is a persistent negative thought pattern. If you find yourselves constantly thinking about worst-case scenarios or dwelling on past failures, it is likely that fear and worry are playing a significant role in your life. By recognizing this negative thought pattern, you can begin to challenge and reframe these thoughts, replacing them with more positive and empowering ones.

Fear and worry can also show up in our relationships. If you notice that you are constantly doubting the intentions and loyalty of others, it may be a sign that fear and worry are impacting your ability to trust. This can hinder personal and romantic relationships, as well as entrepreneurial ventures. By being aware of these patterns, you can work towards building healthier and more fulfilling connections.

Lastly, fear and worry can often be tied to our financial goals. If you find yourselves constantly stressed about money or obsessively checking your bank account, it may be a sign of an unhealthy relationship with money. By recognizing these signs, you can begin to address any underlying fears or limiting beliefs that may be holding you back from achieving your financial goals.

Recognizing the signs and symptoms of fear and worry is the first step towards overcoming them and embracing spiritual transformation. By acknowledging these emotions and their impact on our lives, we can take proactive steps to address them. Whether it is through therapy, meditation, or other self-care practices, it is possible to thrive beyond fear and achieve our goals in all areas of life - be it personal finance, relationships, entrepreneurship, or spiritual growth. Together, let us overcome worry and step into a life of abundance and fulfillment.

The Importance of Overcoming Fear and Worry for Generation X

In a world filled with uncertainties and constant change, it is vital for us to understand the significance of overcoming fear and worry. As individuals who grew up during a time of economic and social transformation, we have faced numerous challenges that have often led to feelings of anxiety, concern, and doubt. However, by embracing the power of overcoming fear and worry, our generation can unlock our true potential and achieve our goals in various aspects of life.

One of the key areas where overcoming worry is crucial is in reaching personal finance goals. We have witnessed economic downturns and market fluctuations, which can create a sense of insecurity about financial stability. By conquering fear and worry, we can develop the confidence to make informed financial decisions, invest wisely, and work toward financial independence.

Moreover, overcoming worry is essential in building and nurturing relationships. Whether it is romantic relationships, friendships, or family bonds, fear and worry can often hinder genuine connections. We must learn to let go of past disappointments, trust others, and have faith in the power of vulnerability.

By overcoming worries related to relationships, we can form deeper connections, experience love, and create a support system that will help us thrive.

For those with entrepreneurial aspirations, fear and worry can be significant barriers to success. Starting a business involves risks, uncertainties, and challenges. However, by embracing courage and overcoming worries related to entrepreneurship, Our generation can turn our dreams into reality. We can embrace failure as a learning opportunity, take calculated risks, and build innovative businesses that shape the future.

Furthermore, overcoming worry is crucial for spiritual and personal growth goals. Our generation has witnessed a decline in traditional religious affiliations, leading many to seek spiritual fulfillment outside of traditional frameworks. By conquering fear and worry, we can explore different spiritual practices, embark on a journey of self-discovery, and find inner peace and purpose.

In conclusion, the importance of overcoming fear and worry for our generation cannot be overstated. By overcoming worries related to personal finance, relationships, entrepreneurship, and spiritual or personal growth, our generation can unlock our full potential and thrive in all aspects of life. It is through conquering fear and embracing courage that our generation can reach our goals, achieve success, and create a life filled with fulfillment and purpose.

CHAPTER 2:
OVERCOMING WORRY TO REACH YOUR GOALS

Setting Clear and Achievable Goals

In order to thrive beyond fear and overcome worry, it is essential for us to set clear and achievable goals. This subchapter delves into the importance of goal setting and provides practical strategies for us to overcome worry and achieve our personal, financial, relationship, entrepreneurial, and spiritual goals.

Setting clear goals is the first step towards overcoming worry and reaching our desired outcomes. By defining what we want to achieve, we provide ourselves with a clear direction and purpose. This clarity helps to alleviate stress and uncertainty, allowing us to focus on taking action towards our goals.

For those who worry about personal finance goals, it

is crucial to establish a realistic financial plan. This may involve setting a budget, reducing debt, increasing savings, or investing wisely. By clearly defining our financial objectives and breaking them down into manageable steps, we can alleviate the worry surrounding money matters and work towards financial stability and success.

Relationship goals can also be a significant source of worry for us. Whether it is finding a life partner, improving an existing relationship, or navigating the complexities of family dynamics, setting clear goals can provide a sense of control and alleviate anxiety. By defining what we desire in our relationships and taking proactive steps towards achieving them, we can cultivate healthier and more fulfilling connections.

Entrepreneurial goals often come with a unique set of worries for us. Whether it is starting a business, expanding a venture, or overcoming obstacles along the way, setting clear and achievable goals is crucial. By breaking down our entrepreneurial aspirations into tangible objectives, we can overcome worry and take strategic steps toward building a successful business.

Finally, for those of us who seek spiritual or personal growth goals, setting clear intentions is vital. Whether it is deepening our spiritual practice, cultivating mindfulness, or embarking on a journey of self-discovery, setting achievable goals can provide structure and guidance. By defining our spiritual or personal growth objectives and committing to regular practices, we can overcome worry and embrace transformational experiences.

In conclusion, setting clear and achievable goals is essential for us to overcome worry and achieve our desired outcomes. By defining what we want to accomplish in various areas of our lives, we can alleviate stress, focus our energy, and take the necessary steps toward success. Whether it is personal, financial, relationship, entrepreneurial, or spiritual goals, the power of goal setting should not be underestimated. Let us embrace the process, commit to our goals, and thrive beyond fear.

Identifying and Addressing the Root Causes of Worry

Worry is a common experience that affects us all, regardless of age or background. As members of Generation X, we find ourselves navigating an increasingly complex and fast-paced world, which can often leave us feeling overwhelmed and burdened by worry. However, to thrive beyond fear and overcome worry, it is essential to identify and address the root causes that trigger these anxieties. In this subchapter, we will explore how to identify and address the root causes of worry, specifically in relation to various aspects of our lives.

For those striving to reach their goals, worry can be a significant obstacle. Whether it be career aspirations, personal development, or financial goals, the fear of failure or the unknown can often hinder our progress. By identifying the underlying beliefs and thought patterns that contribute to our worries, we can begin to challenge and reframe them in a more positive and empowering way.

In the realm of personal finance, worry can consume our thoughts and hinder our ability to make sound financial decisions. The root causes of financial worries include scarcity mentality or past negative experiences. By adopting healthy financial habits, setting realistic goals, and seeking guidance from experts, we can alleviate financial worries and work towards a more secure future.

Relationships play a crucial role in our lives, and worry can often arise when we fear rejection, conflict, or abandonment. Identifying and addressing the root causes of worry in relationships is essential, as it fosters healthier connections and cultivates trust and open communication.

Entrepreneurial goals often come with a unique set of worries, including fear of failure, financial instability, and the uncertainty of the market. By identifying and addressing the root causes of worry in entrepreneurship, we will learn strategies to manage risks, build resilience, and embrace a growth mindset.

Lastly, in the realm of spiritual and personal growth goals, worry can hinder our progress in self-discovery and transformation. By identifying the root causes of worry in this domain, such as fear of the unknown or resistance to change, we can develop spiritual practices, mindfulness techniques, and self-reflection exercises to address and overcome these worries.

In conclusion, identifying and addressing the root causes of worry is essential for overcoming fear and embracing spiritual transformation. By exploring the specific contexts of overcoming worry related to goals, personal finance, relationships, entrepreneurship, and spiritual growth, we have learned practical tools and insights to help our generation thrive beyond fear and embrace a life of fulfillment and purpose.

Developing a Positive Mindset to Combat Worry

In today's fast-paced and uncertain world, it is all too easy for worry to consume our thoughts and sabotage our goals. As members of Generation X, we often find ourselves juggling multiple responsibilities and facing unique challenges. From personal finance and relationships to entrepreneurial ventures and spiritual growth, the worries can seem never-ending. However, by developing a positive mindset, we can combat worry and unlock our true potential.

One of the first steps towards developing a positive mindset is recognizing that worry is a natural human response to uncertainty. It is important to acknowledge our worries and not dismiss them as insignificant. By facing our fears head-on, we can gain a better understanding of what is truly bothering us and take proactive steps to address them.

To combat worry, it is crucial to cultivate a sense of gratitude and focus on the positive aspects of our lives. Our generation has experienced numerous challenges and setbacks, but we have also achieved remarkable successes. By shifting our focus to what is going well, we can reframe our worries and gain a renewed perspective.

Another powerful tool in developing a positive mindset is practicing self-care. Taking care of our physical, mental, and emotional well-being is essential for overcoming worry. This may involve incorporating exercise, mindfulness, or relaxation techniques into our daily routine. By nurturing ourselves, we can build resilience and better cope with the challenges that come our way.

Additionally, surrounding ourselves with a supportive network of like-minded individuals can greatly impact our mindset. Connecting with others who share similar goals and aspirations can provide a sense of camaraderie and encouragement. Through sharing experiences and offering support, we can gain new insights and strategies for overcoming worry.

Lastly, embracing a spiritual or personal growth journey can be transformative in combatting worry. By connecting with something greater than ourselves, whether it be through meditation, prayer, or self-reflection, we can find solace and guidance. This connection can help us gain clarity, purpose, and a sense of peace amidst the chaos.

In conclusion, developing a positive mindset is crucial for overcoming worry and achieving our goals. As members of Generation X, we face unique challenges related to personal finance, relationships, entrepreneurship, and spiritual growth. By acknowledging our worries, cultivating gratitude, practicing self-care, building a supportive network, and embracing a spiritual journey, we can combat worry and thrive in all areas of our lives. Let us embrace this opportunity to transcend fear, overcome worry, and embrace the transformative power within us.

Cultivating Resilience and Persistence in Pursuing Goals

In our journey towards personal growth and achievement, it is not uncommon to encounter various obstacles and setbacks that can dampen our spirits and shake our confidence. However, we possess the inherent qualities of resilience and persistence that can help us overcome these challenges and continue pursuing our goals.

One area where resilience and persistence are essential is in overcoming worry to reach our goals. Often, worry can paralyze us, preventing us from taking the necessary steps towards our aspirations. By cultivating resilience, we can learn to acknowledge our worries and fears while still pushing forward, embracing discomfort and uncertainty as part of the growth process.

Personal finance goals can also be a source of worry for many of us. Whether it's saving for retirement, paying off debt, or achieving financial independence, the journey is rarely smooth. Through resilience, we can develop the mindset to face financial setbacks head-on, learn from our mistakes, and adapt our strategies to ultimately achieve our objectives.

Relationship goals, too, can be a significant source of worry and anxiety. Whether it's finding a life partner, mending a broken relationship, or nurturing existing connections, resilience and persistence are vital. By remaining steadfast in our pursuit of healthy and fulfilling relationships, even in the face of rejection or heartbreak, we can cultivate the resilience necessary to overcome worry and ultimately find the love and connection we seek.

For those of us with entrepreneurial goals, the path to success is often filled with uncertainty and risk. By embracing resilience and persistence, we can bounce back from failures, learn from our experiences, and adapt our strategies to navigate the ever-changing business landscape. This mindset allows us to overcome worry and continue striving towards our entrepreneurial dreams.

Finally, resilience is crucial in attaining spiritual or personal growth goals. This journey often requires us to confront our deepest fears, question our beliefs, and step out of our comfort zones. By cultivating resilience and persistence, we can push through the doubts and fears that arise, allowing us to embrace spiritual transformation and experience personal growth on a profound level.

In conclusion, cultivating resilience and persistence is essential for overcoming worry and achieving our goals in various aspects of life. As members of Generation X, we possess the strength and determination to face challenges head-on, adapt to setbacks, and continue pursuing our dreams. By harnessing these qualities, we can thrive beyond fear, overcome worry, and embrace the spiritual transformation necessary to lead fulfilling and purposeful lives.

CHAPTER 3:
OVERCOMING WORRY RELATED TO PERSONAL FINANCE GOALS

Understanding the Relationship Between Worry and Personal Finances

In our journey toward personal and spiritual growth, one aspect that often holds us back is worry. As members of Generation X, we are no strangers to the challenges and stressors that life throws our way. From financial burdens to relationship struggles, from entrepreneurial pursuits to spiritual growth, worry can infiltrate every aspect of our lives. However, when it comes to our personal finances, worry can have a particularly damaging effect.

Worrying about our financial situation can hinder our progress and prevent us from reaching our goals. It consumes our thoughts, drains our energy, and holds us back from taking the necessary steps toward financial stability and success. But why does this happen? What is the relationship between worry and personal finances?

First and foremost, worry often stems from a fear of the unknown. We may worry about not having enough money to pay our bills or provide for our families. We may fear losing our jobs or being unable to retire comfortably. These concerns can lead to a constant state of anxiety, making it difficult to focus on finding solutions and taking positive action.

Additionally, worry can lead to poor financial decision-making. When we are consumed by fear and uncertainty, we may make impulsive choices that are not in our best interest. We may overspend, accumulate debt, or avoid necessary financial planning and investments. These decisions can further exacerbate our worries and keep us trapped in a cycle of financial insecurity.

To overcome worry related to personal finance goals, we must first acknowledge and understand our fears.

By identifying the specific worries that are holding us back, we can begin to confront and address them head-on. This may involve seeking professional help, such as financial advisors or therapists, who can guide us in creating a solid financial plan and managing our worries effectively.

Moreover, practicing mindfulness and cultivating a positive mindset can greatly impact our relationship with worry and personal finances. By focusing on the present moment and maintaining a sense of gratitude for what we have, we can shift our perspective and reduce anxiety about the future. This can empower us to make thoughtful financial decisions and take proactive steps toward our goals.

Ultimately, overcoming worry related to personal finances is essential for our overall well-being and success. By understanding the relationship between worry and financial stability, we can break free from the cycle of anxiety and embrace a future of abundance and prosperity. It is through this transformation that we can truly thrive beyond fear and achieve our greatest potential.

Assessing and Managing Financial Risks

In today's fast-paced and uncertain world, financial worries can easily become a significant source of stress and anxiety. However, it is essential to understand that overcoming worry related to personal finance goals is not only possible but also crucial for achieving overall success and well-being. In this subchapter, we will delve into the various aspects of assessing and managing financial risks to help us thrive beyond fear and embrace spiritual transformation.

When it comes to assessing financial risks, the first step is to gain clarity about our current financial situation. This involves evaluating our income, expenses, debts, and investments. By having a clear understanding of our financial standing, we can identify potential risks and make informed decisions to mitigate them.

One of the primary concerns for us is planning for retirement. It is essential to assess the risks associated with our retirement savings, such as market volatility and inflation. By diversifying our investments and regularly reviewing our retirement plan, we can mitigate these risks and ensure a secure future.

Another aspect of managing financial risks is overcoming worries related to personal finance goals. Many of us may have concerns about debt, such as student loans or mortgages. By creating a budget, setting financial goals, and adopting healthy spending habits, we can develop a plan to pay off debt and achieve financial freedom.

Additionally, financial worries can also impact relationship goals. It is crucial to have open and honest conversations about money with your partner or spouse. By establishing shared financial goals, creating a joint budget, and regularly reviewing our progress, we can overcome worry and strengthen our relationship.

For those of us with entrepreneurial goals, managing financial risks is vital for success. This includes understanding the financial implications of starting a business, such as securing funding, managing cash flow, and anticipating potential risks. By developing a comprehensive business plan and seeking professional advice, we can mitigate financial risks and increase the likelihood of entrepreneurial success.

Finally, overcoming worry related to spiritual or personal growth goals is essential for overall well-being. Financial worries can often hinder personal growth and spiritual transformation. By developing a mindset of abundance, practicing gratitude, and seeking guidance from spiritual teachings, we can overcome worry and align our financial goals with our spiritual and personal growth aspirations.

In conclusion, assessing and managing financial risks is a crucial aspect of overcoming worry and embracing spiritual transformation for us. By gaining clarity about our financial situation, setting goals, and adopting healthy financial habits, we can mitigate financial risks and achieve overall success and well-being. Remember, with the right mindset and a proactive approach, we can thrive beyond fear and reach our full potential.

Creating a Budget and Financial Plan to Alleviate Worry

In today's fast-paced and uncertain world, it's no wonder that many of us are burdened with worry. Whether it's about reaching personal finance goals, relationship goals, entrepreneurial goals, or even spiritual and personal growth goals, worry can be a significant hindrance to our overall well-being and success. However, by taking control of our financial situation through creating a budget and financial plan, we can alleviate some of this worry and pave the way for a brighter future.

One of the primary sources of worry for our generation is personal finance. Many of us are juggling multiple financial responsibilities, such as mortgages, student loans, and retirement savings. The constant worry about making ends meet and reaching financial goals can be overwhelming. By creating a detailed budget, we can gain clarity on our income and expenses, enabling us to make informed decisions about our spending habits and prioritize our financial goals. Additionally, a financial plan that includes strategies for saving and investing can provide a roadmap toward long-term financial security, alleviating worry and providing peace of mind.

Relationships, both personal and professional, also play a significant role in our overall well-being. The worries associated with maintaining healthy relationships can be challenging, but having a financial plan in place can help alleviate some of this stress. By budgeting for date nights, vacations, or even therapy sessions, we can prioritize our relationships and ensure that we are investing time and resources into nurturing them. Additionally, having a financial plan in place can provide a sense of stability and security in our relationships, reducing worry and allowing us to focus on building meaningful connections.

Entrepreneurial goals often come with their own set of worries. Starting a new business or pursuing a passion project can be financially risky, leading to anxieties about money and stability. By creating a budget and financial plan that includes contingencies for unexpected expenses and a realistic timeline for reaching profitability, we can alleviate some of these worries and approach our entrepreneurial goals with confidence. Having a solid financial foundation can also provide the freedom to take calculated risks and seize opportunities, empowering us to reach our entrepreneurial dreams.

Lastly, overcoming worry related to spiritual or personal growth goals is essential for overall well-being and fulfillment. By creating a budget that includes resources for personal development, such as books, workshops, or retreats, we can invest in our spiritual and personal growth. Having a financial plan in place can also alleviate worries about financial stability, allowing us to focus on our inner journey and embrace spiritual transformation.

In conclusion, creating a budget and financial plan is a powerful tool to alleviate worries and reach our goals across various aspects of life. Whether it's personal finance, relationships, entrepreneurship, or spiritual and personal growth, having a clear financial roadmap empowers us to make informed decisions, prioritize our goals, and ultimately thrive beyond fear.

Building a Strong Financial Foundation for the Future

In today's fast-paced and unpredictable world, it is crucial for us to build a strong financial foundation for the future. As we navigate through various life goals, such as personal finance, relationships, entrepreneurship, and spiritual growth, it is natural to feel anxious and worried about the uncertainties that lie ahead. However, by adopting a proactive approach and embracing key strategies, we can overcome worry and pave the way for a prosperous future.

When it comes to personal finance goals, the first step is to prioritize financial stability. This involves creating a budget, tracking expenses, and saving for emergencies. By keeping a close eye on our finances, we can alleviate worries about unexpected expenses and focus on achieving our long-term financial goals. Additionally, seeking professional advice, such as consulting a financial advisor or attending financial literacy workshops, can provide valuable insights and guidance to enhance our financial well-being.

Relationship goals are an essential part of our lives, but they can also be a significant source of worry. Whether it's maintaining healthy relationships with family, friends, or partners, open communication is key. By expressing our concerns, setting boundaries, and actively listening to others, we can alleviate worry and foster strong connections. Seeking support from therapists or relationship counselors can also provide valuable tools to overcome worry and strengthen our relationships.

Entrepreneurial goals often come with a unique set of worries. Fear of failure, financial instability, and un-certainty can hinder our progress. However, by embracing a growth mindset and focusing on continuous learning, we can overcome these worries. Surrounding ourselves with a network of mentors and like-minded individuals can provide support, guidance, and encouragement on our entrepreneurial journey.

While striving for success in various aspects of life, it is essential not to neglect our spiritual or personal growth goals. Taking time for self¬reflection, meditation, or engaging in activities that bring us joy can nurture our spiritual well-being. By embracing spirituality, we can find solace, purpose, and a sense of peace that helps us overcome worry and navigate the challenges we face

In conclusion, building a strong financial foundation for the future requires a proactive approach and the willingness to overcome worry. By prioritizing financial stability, fostering healthy relationships, embracing entrepreneurship, and nurturing our spiritual growth, we can thrive beyond fear and embrace a transformative and prosperous future. Let go of worry, embrace the possibilities, and embark on a journey toward a life of abundance and fulfillment.

Seeking Professional Help and Resources for Financial Worries

In our journey towards overcoming worry and embracing spiritual transformation, it is crucial to acknowledge that financial concerns can often be a significant source of anxiety. Whether it's striving to reach personal finance goals, navigating the complexities of relationship dynamics, pursuing entrepreneurial endeavors, or seeking spiritual and personal growth, we face unique challenges that can lead to financial worry. However, it is essential to remember that we do not have to face these concerns alone.

One of the most effective ways to address financial worries is to seek professional help and utilize available resources. Financial advisors, counselors, and coaches can provide valuable guidance and support, offering insights tailored to our specific goals and circumstances. These professionals have the expertise to help us develop effective strategies, manage our finances, and alleviate the burden of worry.

When it comes to personal finance goals, seeking professional help can help us create a comprehensive plan to achieve financial stability, whether it involves budgeting, debt management, or investment strategies. By working closely with a financial advisor, we can gain clarity and confidence in making sound financial decisions, enabling us to overcome worry and focus on reaching our goals.

In the realm of relationship goals, financial worries can often strain our connections with loved ones. Seeking the assistance of a relationship counselor or therapist can provide a safe space to address these concerns.

These professionals can guide us in navigating difficult conversations about money, fostering open communication, and developing healthy financial habits within our relationships. By addressing these worries head-on, we can strengthen our bonds and work towards shared financial objectives.

For those pursuing entrepreneurial goals, professional help can be invaluable in managing the financial aspects of starting and growing a business. Accountants, business coaches, and mentors can provide crucial insights into financial planning, budgeting, cash flow management, and tax strategies. By leveraging their expertise, we can alleviate worry and focus on building a thriving entrepreneurial venture.

Finally, as we strive for spiritual and personal growth, financial worries can hinder our progress. Seeking guidance from spiritual leaders, life coaches, or therapists with a focus on personal development can help us explore the underlying beliefs and emotions that contribute to financial worry. By addressing these deeper issues, we can cultivate a mindset of abundance, shift our perspectives, and embrace spiritual transformation.

Remember, seeking professional help and utilizing available resources is not a sign of weakness but rather a courageous step toward overcoming financial worries. By leveraging the expertise and support of professionals, we can navigate the challenges specific to our goals and circumstances, empowering us to thrive beyond fear and embrace the spiritual transformation we desire.

CHAPTER 4:
OVERCOMING WORRY RELATED TO RELATIONSHIP GOALS

In the journey of personal growth and transformation, relationships play a pivotal role. Whether it is romantic relationships, friendships, or even professional connections, our interactions with others have the power to shape our lives and contribute to our overall well-being. However, it is not uncommon for fear and worry to creep into the realm of relationships, hindering our ability to form meaningful connections and achieve our goals.

In this chapter, we will delve deep into the intricacies of fear and worry in relationship settings, specifically addressing the concerns of our generation. As members of this unique generation, we often find ourselves grappling with a myriad of worries related to our personal and professional lives, and relationships are no exception.

Examining Fear and Worry in Relationship Settings

One common worry that many of us face is the fear of opening up and being vulnerable in relationships. The fear of rejection and the uncertainty of how others will perceive us can hold us back from forming deep and meaningful connections. We will explore strategies and techniques to overcome these fears, allowing us to nurture healthy and fulfilling relationships.

Furthermore, personal finance goals often intertwine with our relationships, leading to additional worries and anxieties. Whether it is concerns about financial stability or the fear of being taken advantage of, we will explore practical solutions to overcome these worries and find a balance between financial aspirations and healthy relationships.

Entrepreneurial goals can also be impacted by fear

and worry in relationship settings. Fear of failure, fear of rejection, and fear of judgment from others can hinder our ability to take risks and pursue our entrepreneurial dreams. By examining these fears and providing actionable steps, we will empower our generation to overcome these obstacles and thrive in our entrepreneurial pursuits.

Lastly, we will address the role of fear and worry in spiritual or personal growth goals. Many of us seek spiritual enlightenment and personal growth, but fear and worry can act as barriers on this transformative journey. Through mindfulness practices, self-reflection, and embracing vulnerability, we will guide readers to overcome these fears and embrace spiritual transformation.

In conclusion, fear and worry are natural aspects of the human experience, but they should not dictate our relationships and hinder our personal growth. By understanding the specific fears and worries that we face in relationship settings, we can equip ourselves with the tools and knowledge necessary to thrive beyond fear. Let us embark on this transformative journey together, embracing vulnerability and creating the meaningful connections we desire.

Enhancing Communication and Trust to Reduce Worry

In our fast-paced and constantly evolving world, we face unique challenges when it comes to overcoming worry and reaching our goals. From personal finance to relationships, entrepreneurship to spiritual growth, the pressures can feel overwhelming at times. However, by focusing on enhancing communication and building trust, we can effectively reduce worry and embrace a positive transformation in our lives.

One of the key factors in overcoming worry is effective communication. In our personal relationships, open and honest communication is essential. By expressing our fears, concerns, and goals to our loved ones, we create a support system that can help us navigate through difficult times. Similarly, in our professional endeavors and entrepreneurial pursuits, clear and concise communication with colleagues, partners, and clients is vital. By openly discussing challenges and seeking feedback, we can build trust and foster an environment of collaboration and support.

Trust is another essential element in reducing worry and achieving our goals. By cultivating trust in ourselves, we can develop confidence in our abilities and decision-making. This self-trust allows us to take risks and embrace opportunities without fear of failure. Additionally, building trust with others is crucial. Surrounding ourselves with reliable and supportive individuals who share our vision and values can help alleviate worries and provide the necessary encouragement to pursue our goals.

When it comes to personal finance, effective communication and trust are paramount. By openly discussing our financial concerns and goals with a partner or financial advisor, we can develop a solid plan to overcome financial worries and work towards our aspirations. Building trust in our financial decisions and staying committed to our financial goals will help ease worries and pave the way for a more secure future.

In our spiritual or personal growth journey, communication and trust play a vital role as well. By seeking support from like-minded individuals or joining spiritual communities, we can share our worries and receive guidance and inspiration. Trusting the process and having faith in our own spiritual transformation allows us to embrace the uncertainties and challenges that come with personal growth.

In conclusion, enhancing communication and building trust are powerful tools for reducing worry and achieving our goals. By openly communicating our fears, concerns, and aspirations, we create a support system that can guide us through challenges. Trusting ourselves and those around us fosters confidence, collaboration, and a positive environment for growth. Whether it's in personal finance, relationships, entrepreneurship, or spiritual development, these principles can help us thrive beyond fear and embrace the transformative journey toward a fulfilling life.

Nurturing Healthy Boundaries and Self-Care in Relationships

In our fast-paced and interconnected world, it is crucial for us to prioritize our own well-being and establish healthy boundaries in our relationships. In this subchapter, we delve into the importance of maintaining healthy boundaries and practicing self-care in various aspects of life.

One area where healthy boundaries are essential is in overcoming worry to reach our goals. We often find ourselves overwhelmed by worries and fears that hinder our progress. By setting healthy boundaries, such as limiting exposure to negative influences or toxic relationships, we can create a supportive environment that fosters personal growth and allows us to focus on our goals with clarity and determination.

Moreover, many of us face anxiety and stress when it comes to managing our finances. By establishing healthy boundaries around spending habits, saving strategies, and seeking professional advice when needed, we can alleviate financial worries and work towards achieving our long-term financial goals.

Relationships play a vital role in our lives, and it is essential to address the worry associated with relationship goals. Setting healthy boundaries in romantic partnerships, friendships, and family dynamics is essential. By nurturing healthy boundaries, we can foster healthier and more fulfilling relationships, allowing us to thrive personally and emotionally.

Furthermore, we often experience concerns and doubts when starting our own businesses or pursuing entrepreneurial ventures. By setting boundaries around time management, seeking support from mentors or coaches, and maintaining a healthy work-life balance, we can alleviate worries and focus on achieving our entrepreneurial aspirations.

Lastly, we often seek spiritual or personal growth, but worry can hinder our progress. By setting boundaries around self-care practices, nurturing a supportive community, and engaging in activities that promote spiritual growth, we can overcome worries and embrace transformative experiences.

In conclusion, by prioritizing healthy boundaries and self-care in various aspects of life, we can overcome worries and fears, allowing us to achieve our goals, both personally and professionally.

Resolving Conflict and Addressing Relationship Worries

In our pursuit of thriving beyond fear, it is essential to acknowledge that conflict and relationship worries are inevitable aspects of life. As members of Generation X, we have encountered various challenges in our personal and professional lives, which often lead to feelings of worry and uncertainty. However, it is crucial to understand that these worries can be overcome through effective conflict resolution and addressing relationship concerns.

One area where worry can hinder our progress is in reaching our goals. Whether it is our career aspirations, personal growth, or financial objectives, worry can impede our ability to take necessary risks and move forward. By recognizing and addressing these worries head-on, we can develop strategies to overcome them. This may involve seeking support from mentors or professionals who can guide us through the process and provide valuable insights.

Personal finance goals often create anxiety and worry for many of us. Whether it is managing debt, saving for retirement, or planning for the future, financial concerns can be overwhelming. However, by developing a proactive mindset and seeking financial advice, we can regain control over our financial well-being. Learning practical strategies for budgeting, saving, and investing can alleviate worry and help us achieve our financial goals.

Relationship goals are another area where worry can strain our emotional well-being. Whether it is conflicts with a partner, family member, or friend, addressing relationship worries is crucial to maintaining healthy connections. Open and honest communication, active listening, and empathy are essential tools for conflict resolution. Seeking professional help, such as couples counseling or mediation, can also provide guidance and support in navigating relationship challenges.

For those pursuing entrepreneurial goals, worry can be particularly daunting. The fear of failure, financial instability, or the unknown can hinder our progress. However, understanding that worry is a natural part of the entrepreneurial journey can help alleviate its impact. Developing a strong support network, seeking mentorship, and embracing a growth mindset can empower us to overcome worry and achieve entrepreneurial success.

Finally, addressing worry related to spiritual or personal growth goals is essential for our overall well-being. Cultivating a spiritual practice, whether through meditation, prayer, or self-reflection, can provide solace and clarity. Engaging in personal growth activities, such as attending workshops or seeking guidance from spiritual leaders, can aid in overcoming worry and fostering transformation.

In conclusion, resolving conflict and addressing relationship worries is vital for us in our pursuit of thriving beyond fear. By acknowledging and confronting worries related to our goals, personal finances, relationships, entrepreneurial endeavors, and spiritual growth, we can develop strategies to overcome these concerns. Through open communication, seeking professional support, and adopting a proactive mindset, we can embrace spiritual transformation and overcome worry to reach our full potential.

Seeking Support and Guidance for Relationship Worries

In our journey through life, we often encounter challenges and worries that can leave us feeling overwhelmed and uncertain. One area where worries can be particularly intense is in our relationships. Whether it's a romantic partnership, a friendship, or a family dynamic, the ups and downs of our connections with others can often be a significant source of stress and concern.

Fortunately, there are various avenues to seek support and guidance when it comes to relationship worries. In this subchapter, we will explore how overcoming worry in relationships can help us thrive beyond fear and embrace spiritual transformation. We will delve into specific niches within our generation, including overcoming worry to reach personal finance goals, relationship goals, entrepreneurial goals, and spiritual or personal growth goals.

When facing relationship worries, it is crucial to remember that seeking support is not a sign of weakness but rather a sign of strength and self-awareness. One avenue to consider is professional counseling or therapy. A trained therapist can provide a safe space for you to express your concerns, explore underlying issues, and develop strategies for improving your relationships. They can guide you in understanding patterns and communication styles and offer valuable tools to overcome worry and achieve your goals.

For those specifically seeking support in overcoming worry related to personal finance goals, financial advisors and coaches can offer valuable insight and guidance. They can help you develop a solid financial plan, address any concerns or fears around money, and provide strategies for improving your financial situation while maintaining healthy relationships.

In the realm of entrepreneurial goals, mentors and business coaches can be invaluable resources. These experienced professionals can offer guidance on building and maintaining successful business relationships, managing conflicts, and overcoming worry to achieve your entrepreneurial dreams.

When it comes to spiritual or personal growth goals, seeking guidance from spiritual leaders and mentors or attending workshops and retreats can provide a nurturing environment for reflection and growth. These experiences can help you gain clarity, develop a deeper understanding of yourself and your relationships, and find inner peace.

In conclusion, seeking support and guidance for relationship worries is essential for us to overcome worry and embrace spiritual transformation. Whether it's

through therapy, financial advisors, mentors, or spiritual leaders, there are numerous resources available
to help you navigate the challenges of relationships
and achieve your goals. By seeking support, you can
thrive beyond fear and build fulfilling and meaningful connections with others.

CHAPTER 5:
OVERCOMING WORRY RELATED TO ENTREPRENEURIAL GOALS

Understanding the Challenges and Risks of Entrepreneurship

Entrepreneurship is an exhilarating journey that offers the potential for personal and financial growth. However, it is not without its fair share of challenges and risks. Whether you are a part of Generation X or any other generation, understanding these obstacles is crucial for navigating the entrepreneurial landscape successfully.

One of the primary challenges of entrepreneurship is the uncertainty that comes with starting your own business. Unlike traditional employment, where a steady paycheck and predictable work routine are the norm, entrepreneurship requires you to embrace ambiguity. This uncertainty can cause worry and anxiety, especially for our generation, who may have financial and familial responsibilities.

Financial risks are another significant concern for entrepreneurs. Starting a business often requires a substantial investment of money, time, and resources. There is always a possibility of financial loss, especially in the early stages when the business is still finding its footing. This can be particularly worrisome for us, who may be hesitant to take financial risks due to our focus on stability and security.

Entrepreneurship also demands a significant commitment of time and energy. Building a successful business requires long hours, sacrifices, and the ability to handle multiple responsibilities simultaneously. Balancing personal and professional life can be challenging, leading to worry related to relationships and personal growth goals. Some of us who may be juggling family, work, and personal aspirations may find it especially challenging to find harmony in our lives.

Additionally, entrepreneurship can pose risks to one's spiritual or personal growth goals. The pressure to succeed, coupled with the fear of failure, can overshadow the pursuit of personal fulfillment and spiritual well-being. Some of us who value personal growth and spirituality may need to find ways to integrate these aspects into our entrepreneurial journey to maintain balance and overcome worry.

In conclusion, understanding the challenges and risks of entrepreneurship is essential for those of us who are pursuing entrepreneurial goals. By acknowledging and addressing the uncertainties, financial risks, time commitments, and potential impact on personal growth and relationships, entrepreneurs can better navigate the journey and overcome worry. Embracing a mindset of resilience and adaptability and seeking support from mentors and like-minded individuals can help us thrive beyond fear and achieve our goals.

Embracing Failure and Learning from Setbacks

In the journey towards personal growth and achieving our goals, setbacks and failures are inevitable. They can be discouraging and disheartening, often leading us to doubt our abilities and question our purpose. However, it is during these moments of adversity that we have the chance to truly learn and grow.

For our generation, a generation known for its resilience and determination, embracing failure can be a powerful tool for overcoming worry and reaching our goals. Whether it's in our personal finances, relationships, entrepreneurial ventures, or spiritual growth, setbacks can offer valuable lessons that propel us forward.

When it comes to overcoming worries related to personal finance goals, failure can teach us the importance of financial literacy and planning. It reminds us to set realistic expectations, save for unforeseen circumstances, and seek advice from experts. By embracing failure, we can learn from our financial mistakes and make wiser decisions in the future.

In relationships, setbacks can teach us the value of communication, empathy, and compromise. By acknowledging our failures, we can learn from them and build healthier, stronger connections with others. Embracing failure in relationships also means letting go of fear and vulnerability, allowing us to cultivate deeper and more meaningful connections.

Entrepreneurial goals often come with a fair share of failures, but they also offer invaluable learning opportunities. Embracing failure in entrepreneurship means being willing to take risks, adapt to changes, and learn from our mistakes. By doing so, we can develop resilience, problem-solving skills, and the ability to bounce back stronger than ever before.

Lastly, embracing failure in our spiritual or personal growth goals allows us to develop a deeper understanding of ourselves and our purpose. It teaches us the importance of self-reflection, perseverance, and humility. Through setbacks, we can explore new paths, question our beliefs, and ultimately embark on a journey toward spiritual transformation.

In conclusion, by understanding that failure is not the end but rather a stepping stone toward growth, we can overcome worry and achieve our goals in all areas of life. So, let us embrace failure, learn from our setbacks, and thrive beyond fear.

Managing Financial Worries in Entrepreneurship

Entrepreneurship can be an exciting and fulfilling journey, but it also comes with its fair share of financial worries. As a Generation X entrepreneur, it is crucial to understand how to manage these worries effectively to ensure your success and reach your goals. In this subchapter, we will explore various strategies to overcome financial worries and thrive in your entrepreneurial endeavors.

One of the primary concerns for entrepreneurs is personal finance. It is essential to overcome worry related to personal finance goals to maintain financial stability. Start by creating a realistic budget that aligns with your business income and expenses. This will help you track your financial progress and identify areas where adjustments are needed. Consider consulting with a financial advisor who specializes in working with entrepreneurs to gain valuable insights and guidance.

In addition to personal finance, entrepreneurs often worry about relationship goals. Balancing work and personal relationships can be challenging, but it is crucial for overall well-being. Communicate openly with your loved ones about your entrepreneurial journey and set realistic expectations. Find ways to prioritize quality time with family and friends, as it can help alleviate worries and strengthen these relationships.

Entrepreneurs also face worries related to their entrepreneurial goals. It is essential to manage these worries by breaking down your goals into smaller, actionable steps. Set clear milestones and celebrate each achievement along the way. Surround yourself with a supportive network of mentors, fellow entrepreneurs, and industry experts who can provide guidance and encouragement.

In conclusion, managing financial worries in entrepreneurship requires a multifaceted approach. By addressing personal finance goals, nurturing relationships, setting achievable milestones, and prioritizing spiritual and personal growth, entrepreneurs in our generation can overcome worry and thrive in our entrepreneurial journeys. Embrace these strategies and let go of fear to unlock your full potential and achieve lasting success.

Building a Support Network and Seeking Mentorship

In our journey towards overcoming worry and embracing spiritual transformation, one vital aspect we often overlook is the power of building a strong support network and seeking mentorship. As members of Generation X, we have faced our fair share of challenges and have witnessed the rapid pace of change in various aspects of life. However, by cultivating a network of like-minded individuals and seeking guidance from mentors, we can navigate these uncertainties with confidence, clarity, and purpose.

One area where a support network can be particularly impactful is in overcoming worry to reach our goals. Whether it's career aspiration, personal development objective, or financial milestone, having a group of individuals who believe in our potential can provide the encouragement and motivation we need to push through self-doubt and anxiety. Surrounding ourselves with positive influences can help us stay focused on our goals and remind us of our capabilities, even when the road ahead seems daunting.

Speaking of personal finance goals, the worry associated with managing finances is a common concern for many of us. Building a support network that includes individuals with expertise in financial planning or investment can be immensely helpful. They can offer guidance on budgeting, saving, and investing, helping us make informed decisions and alleviate financial worries. Additionally, seeking mentorship from successful individuals who have achieved financial stability can provide valuable insights and strategies to overcome financial obstacles.

Relationship goals are another area where worry can often creep in. By connecting with individuals who have experienced successful and fulfilling relationships, we can gain valuable wisdom and advice. A support network can offer a safe space to discuss relationship concerns, seek guidance on communication and conflict resolution, and gain insights into building strong, meaningful connections. Moreover, mentors who have navigated the complexities of relationships can offer valuable guidance, helping us overcome worry and work towards achieving our relationship goals.

For those of us with entrepreneurial goals, building a support network becomes even more crucial. Surrounding ourselves with like-minded individuals who have experience in entrepreneurship can provide invaluable advice, support, and even potential collaborations. Additionally, seeking mentorship from successful entrepreneurs can help us navigate the challenges and uncertainties that come with starting our own ventures. Their guidance, insight, and experiences can help us overcome worry and pave the way for our entrepreneurial success.

Lastly, as we embark on our spiritual or personal growth goals, having a support network that understands and supports our journey is essential. Connecting with individuals who share similar spiritual or personal growth aspirations can provide encouragement, accountability, and a sense of belonging. Additionally, seeking mentorship from individuals who have already undergone significant spiritual or personal transformation can offer guidance, tools, and practices to help us overcome worry and embrace our journey toward self-discovery and spiritual growth.

In conclusion, building a support network and seeking mentorship is crucial for overcoming worry and embracing spiritual transformation for our generation. By surrounding ourselves with individuals who believe in our potential, seeking guidance from mentors who have achieved success in various areas, and connecting with like-minded individuals, we can overcome worries related to reaching our goals, personal finance, relationships, entrepreneurship, and spiritual or personal growth. Together, we can navigate the uncertainties of life with confidence, resilience, and a sense of purpose.

Cultivating Resilience and Perseverance in Entrepreneurship

Entrepreneurship is a journey filled with numerous challenges and obstacles. As members of Generation X, we have witnessed the rise and fall of many businesses, which can often lead to worry and apprehension when it comes to pursuing our own entrepreneurial goals. However, it is essential for us to cultivate resilience and perseverance in order to overcome these worries and achieve success.

One of the key aspects of cultivating resilience in entrepreneurship is embracing failure as a learning opportunity. As entrepreneurs, we are bound to face setbacks and encounter failures along the way. Instead of allowing these failures to discourage us, we must view them as valuable lessons that can propel us forward. By adopting a growth mindset and reframing failure as an essential part of the journey, we can bounce back stronger and more determined than ever.

Another crucial aspect of resilience is maintaining a strong support network. Surrounding ourselves with like-minded individuals who understand the unique challenges of entrepreneurship can provide us with the encouragement and guidance needed to persevere. Whether it's joining an entrepreneurial group, seeking out mentors, or connecting with fellow entrepreneurs, having a strong support system can help alleviate worries and provide valuable insights.

In addition to resilience, perseverance is equally important in entrepreneurship. It is natural to face moments of doubt and uncertainty, especially when it comes to personal finance, relationships, spiritual growth, and other areas of our lives. However, it is vital to stay committed to our goals and push through these challenges. By setting clear objectives, creating a solid business plan, and taking consistent action, we can overcome worry and make progress toward our entrepreneurial aspirations.

When it comes to spiritual or personal growth goals, cultivating resilience and perseverance can be deeply transformative. Nurturing our inner selves and developing a strong spiritual foundation can provide us with the strength and clarity needed to navigate the ups and downs of entrepreneurship.

By incorporating practices such as meditation, mindfulness, and self-reflection into our daily routines, we can cultivate resilience and persevere even in the face of adversity.

In conclusion, cultivating resilience and perseverance is essential for overcoming worries and achieving success in entrepreneurship. By embracing failure as a learning opportunity, building a strong support network, and maintaining a sense of determination, entrepreneurs in our generation can overcome worries related to personal finance, relationships, spiritual growth, and other aspects of our lives. With resilience and perseverance, we can thrive beyond fear and embrace the transformative journey of entrepreneurship.

CHAPTER 6:
OVERCOMING WORRY RELATED TO SPIRITUAL OR PERSONAL GROWTH GOALS

Exploring the Relationship Between Worry and Spiritual Growth

In our fast-paced and ever-changing world, our generation faces unique challenges when it comes to achieving personal and spiritual growth. One of the most prevalent obstacles that hinder our progress is worry. Whether it's about reaching our goals, personal finances, relationships, entrepreneurship, or spiritual growth, worry can hold us back from thriving beyond fear and embracing transformation.

Worry is a natural human response to uncertainty and the fear of the unknown. It often stems from the desire to control outcomes and avoid potential failures or disappointments. However, if left unchecked, worry can become a barrier to our spiritual growth and hinder our ability to reach our goals.

On the path to overcoming worry and embracing spiritual transformation, it is essential to understand the relationship between worry and our inner growth. Worry can become a consuming force that distracts us from tapping into our inner potential and connecting with our higher purpose. It can drain our energy, create self-doubt, and erode our faith in ourselves and the divine.

To overcome worry and cultivate spiritual growth, we must first acknowledge and accept our worries. By bringing them into our awareness, we can examine their roots and understand why they hold power over us. This self-reflection allows us to detach from our worries and view them objectively, opening the door to spiritual growth.

Next, we can explore various practices that help us transcend worry and foster spiritual transformation. These practices may include meditation, prayer, mindfulness, journaling, and seeking guidance from wise mentors or spiritual teachers. By engaging in these practices, we can develop a deeper connection with our inner selves and the divine, allowing us to find peace, clarity, and guidance amidst our worries.

Furthermore, it is crucial to cultivate a mindset of trust and surrender. Instead of trying to control every aspect of our lives, we can learn to trust in the unfolding of our journeys and have faith that everything happens for our highest good. By surrendering our worries to a higher power, we free ourselves from the burdens of worry and open ourselves up to spiritual growth and transformation.

In conclusion, worry and spiritual growth are intertwined in the journey of our generation. By acknowledging and understanding our worries, practicing self-reflection and spiritual disciplines, and cultivating trust and surrender, we can overcome worry and embrace spiritual transformation. Through this process, we can achieve our goals, whether they are related to personal finances, relationships, entrepreneurship, or personal growth, and thrive beyond fear, living a life of purpose, fulfillment, and spiritual abundance.

Embracing Mindfulness and Present Moment Awareness

In today's fast-paced and anxiety-inducing world, it is easy for us to become overwhelmed by worry and fear. However, there is a powerful tool that can help us overcome these obstacles and embrace a more fulfilling life - mindfulness and present-moment awareness.

Mindfulness is the practice of intentionally focusing our attention on the present moment without judgment. It allows us to fully experience and engage with our thoughts, emotions, and sensations instead of being caught up in the worries of the past or future. By cultivating mindfulness, we can break free from the chains of worry and find inner peace and clarity.

When it comes to reaching our goals, whether they are related to personal finance, relationships, entrepreneurship, or spiritual growth, worry often acts as a significant barrier. We may worry about not having enough money to achieve our financial goals, fear rejection or failure in our relationships, or doubt our abilities to succeed as entrepreneurs. These worries can paralyze us and prevent us from taking the necessary steps to move forward.

However, by embracing mindfulness and present-moment awareness, we can transform our relationship with worry. Instead of allowing worry to control us, we can observe our worries without judgment, acknowledging their presence but not allowing them to dictate our actions. Mindfulness teaches us that worry is just a passing thought and we have the power to choose how we respond to it.

By practicing mindfulness, we can cultivate a sense of calm and peace within ourselves, even amidst the chaos and uncertainty of life. We can develop the ability to tune into the present moment, appreciating the beauty and opportunities that exist right now. This heightened awareness allows us to make conscious decisions and take intentional actions toward our goals rather than being driven by worry and fear.

Cultivating a Spiritual Practice to Alleviate Worry

In our fast-paced and ever-changing world, it is no surprise that worry has become a common companion for many individuals, especially those belonging to our generation. As we navigate the challenges of reaching our goals in various areas of life - be it personal finance, relationships, entrepreneurship, or spiritual and personal growth, worry can often hinder our progress and hold us back from achieving our true potential.

One powerful tool that our generation can harness to alleviate worry is the cultivation of a spiritual practice. By integrating spirituality into our daily lives, we can develop a sense of inner peace, clarity, and resilience that enables us to overcome worry and thrive beyond fear.

When it comes to overcoming worry and reaching our goals, the foundation of a spiritual practice lies in mindfulness. By practicing present-moment awareness, we can detach ourselves from the incessant chatter of our minds and become more attuned to the present reality. This allows us to shift our focus from worrying about the future or dwelling on the past to fully engaging with the opportunities and challenges that arise in the present moment.

Furthermore, a spiritual practice can provide us with a sense of purpose and meaning in our lives. By connecting with something greater than ourselves - whether it be a higher power, the universe, or our own inner wisdom, we can tap into a source of guidance and inspiration. This connection helps us navigate the uncertainties and setbacks that come along the way, reminding us that we are not alone and that there is a greater purpose to our journey.

In the context of personal finance goals, a spiritual practice can help us develop a healthy relationship with money and detach our self-worth from our financial status. By cultivating gratitude for what we have, practicing mindful spending, and letting go of the need for excessive material possessions, we can alleviate the worry and stress often associated with money.

In relationships, a spiritual practice can teach us the importance of empathy, forgiveness, and unconditional love. By embracing these qualities, we can overcome worry related to conflicts, misunderstandings, and the fear of rejection, fostering deeper connections and nurturing healthy, fulfilling relationships.

For those pursuing entrepreneurial goals, a spiritual practice can offer solace during times of uncertainty and failure. By embracing the mindset of abundance, trusting in our own abilities, and surrendering to the flow of life, we can overcome worry related to financial risks, competition, and the fear of failure. This allows us to approach entrepreneurship with a sense of resilience, creativity, and innovation.

Lastly, for those seeking spiritual or personal growth, a spiritual practice provides a framework for self-reflection, self-discovery, and self-compassion. By engaging in practices such as meditation, prayer, journaling, or engaging in nature, we can deepen our connection with our true selves and tap into our innate wisdom. This helps us overcome worry related to self-doubt, comparison, and the fear of not living up to our potential.

In conclusion, cultivating a spiritual practice is a powerful tool that our generation can embrace to alleviate worry and thrive beyond fear. By incorporating mindfulness, purpose, and connection into our lives, we can overcome worries related to personal finance, relationships, entrepreneurship, and spiritual or personal growth goals. Through the cultivation of spiritual practice, we can find the inner strength, resilience, and peace needed to navigate the challenges of life and truly thrive.

Letting Go of Fear and Surrendering to Divine Guidance

In our fast-paced and often chaotic world, fear has become an all-too-familiar companion for many of us. Whether it's the fear of failure, the fear of rejection, or the fear of the unknown, these anxieties can hold us back from reaching our full potential and achieving our goals. However, it is possible to break free from the grip of fear and embrace a life guided by divine wisdom and intuition.

When we allow fear to dominate our thoughts, we limit ourselves and hinder our progress. It's time to let go of fear and surrender to divine guidance. By doing so, we can tap into a source of infinite wisdom that will support us in overcoming worry and embracing spiritual transformation.

One of the key ways to release fear is by cultivating trust in the Universe or a higher power. By surrendering our worries and fears to this higher power, we acknowledge that there is a greater plan at work and that we are not alone in our journey. This trust allows us to let go of the need to control every aspect of our lives and, instead, surrender to the flow of life.

Overcoming worry related to personal finance goals is a common concern for many of us. By surrendering our fears of scarcity and lack to divine guidance, we can tap into the abundance that the Universe has to offer. Trusting in divine guidance can help us make wise financial decisions and attract the opportunities and resources we need to thrive.

For those pursuing entrepreneurial goals, fear of failure can be paralyzing. By surrendering these fears to divine guidance, we can tap into our inner wisdom and intuition, making decisions from a place of alignment and authenticity. Trusting in divine guidance can also help us overcome the fear of taking risks and embrace the opportunities that come our way.

Finally, in our quest for spiritual and personal growth, fear can hold us back from stepping into our true potential. By surrendering our fears to divine guidance, we can let go of limiting beliefs and step into our power. Trusting in the divine plan allows us to embrace the journey of self-discovery and transformation, knowing that we are guided and supported every step of the way.

In conclusion, letting go of fear and surrendering to divine guidance is essential for overcoming worry and embracing spiritual transformation in life. By cultivating trust in a higher power, we can release our fears and anxieties, allowing us to reach our goals in personal finance, relationships, entrepreneurship, and spiritual growth. Letting go of fear and surrendering to divine guidance is the key to thriving beyond fear and living a life of abundance, love, and fulfillment.

CONCLUSION: EMBRACING SPIRITUAL TRANS-FORMATION FOR GENERATION X

Throughout this book, we have delved into various aspects of our lives that often cause us worry and hinder our ability to reach our goals. However, we have also discovered the power of spiritual transformation in overcoming these worries and unlocking our true potential.

For our generation, a generation marked by rapid technological advancements and societal changes, overcoming worry is essential to finding fulfillment and success in all areas of life. Whether it is related to personal finance, relationships, entrepreneurship, or personal growth, our worries can hold us back and prevent us from taking the necessary steps toward achieving our goals.

One of the key insights we have explored is that spiritual transformation is not limited to religious beliefs or practices. It is a profound shift in mindset and perspective that allows us to see beyond our worries and tap into a deeper sense of purpose and inner strength. By embracing spiritual transformation, we can cultivate resilience, find peace amidst chaos, and develop a strong sense of self-belief.

In the realm of personal finance goals, our worries often revolve around scarcity, debt, and the fear of financial instability. However, by embracing spiritual transformation, we can shift our focus from lack to abundance, make wise financial decisions, and attract opportunities that align with our goals.

When it comes to relationship goals, worries about rejection, heartbreak, and loneliness can hinder us from forming meaningful connections. Through spiritual transformation, we can cultivate love, compassion, and forgiveness, enabling us to build healthier and more fulfilling relationships.

Entrepreneurial goals often come with worries about failure, competition, and financial risks. By embracing spiritual transformation, we can tap into our creativity and intuition, overcome fear, and navigate the challenges of entrepreneurship with resilience and determination.

Lastly, in the pursuit of spiritual or personal growth goals, worries about self-doubt, lack of progress, and the fear of the unknown can often hold us back. However, through spiritual transformation, we can cultivate self-awareness, practice mindfulness, and embrace the transformative power of self-reflection and personal growth.

In conclusion, embracing spiritual transformation is a powerful tool for us to overcome worries and reach our goals. By shifting our mindset, developing inner strength, and aligning with a higher purpose, we can transcend our worries and thrive in all areas of life. Remember, you have the power to overcome fear and embrace spiritual transformation to unlock your fullest potential.

APPENDIX: RESOURCES FOR OVERCOMING WORRY AND EMBRACING SPIRITUAL TRANSFORMATION

In this appendix, we provide a comprehensive list of resources to help you overcome worry and embrace spiritual transformation. These resources are specifically tailored to the needs and interests of our generation, addressing various aspects of life such as personal finance, relationships, entrepreneurship, and spiritual or personal growth goals. Whether you are struggling with worry in these areas or simply seeking guidance to enhance your journey, these resources will serve as valuable tools to support you.

1. Books on Overcoming Worry: Explore literature that delves into the psychology of worry and provides practical strategies to overcome it. Some highly recommended titles include "The Worry Cure" by Robert L. Leahy and "Don't Sweat the Small Stuff...and It's All Small Stuff" by Richard Carlson.

2. Financial Planning and Management: Overcome worries related to personal finance goals by accessing resources that offer financial planning advice, tips for budgeting, and strategies for wealth management. Websites like The Motley Fool and Investopedia provide comprehensive information on these topics.

3. Relationship Coaching and Counseling: If worry is affecting your relationships, consider seeking guidance from relationship coaches or professional counselors. Websites like *Psychology Today* and *BetterHelp* offer directories of relationship experts who can provide guidance on communication, conflict resolution, and building healthy relationships.

4. Entrepreneurial Resources: Overcoming worry related to entrepreneurial goals requires a unique set of resources. Websites like Entrepreneur and Inc. offer valuable insights, advice, and success stories from entrepreneurs who have faced and conquered their worries on the path to success.

5. Spiritual and Personal Growth Resources: For those seeking spiritual or personal growth, resources like meditation apps (such as Headspace or Calm) and spiritual development websites (like Gaia or Tiny Buddha) can provide guidance, inspiration, and techniques to overcome worry and foster personal transformation.

Additionally, consider seeking support from local community centers, religious institutions, or mentorship programs that align with your spiritual or personal growth goals. These resources often offer workshops, retreats, and seminars tailored to your needs.

Remember that overcoming worry and embracing spiritual transformation is a unique journey for each individual. It may require a combination of resources, so explore different avenues until you find what resonates with you. The key is to remain open-minded, committed to personal growth, and willing to take the necessary steps to thrive beyond fear and worry.

ABOUT THE AUTHOR

<u>Floyd Jones Sanders</u> is the Principal and Managing Director at P.A.C.E. Family Services, an agency providing anger parenting, anger management Counseling, and Exchange services in California. Floyd graduated from UC Davis with a degree in Analytic Philosophy and History. He is a professional anger management counselor, certified Domestic Violence therapist, and Life Coach. He is certified in the ABCs of Parenting through Yale University. Floyd has over 25 years of experience in the field of individual counseling, coaching, and family services.

He currently lives in Sacramento, California. If you would like more information about coaching/counseling services or the network marketing company Floyd is a part of, or you are interested in becoming a distributor or customer, see the contact information information below.

www.pacefamilyservices.com

www.floydsanders.lifevantage.com

email: floydj.sanders@outlooklook.com

9 789694 292403